WOODCUTS

Nicholas Sperakis

SMYRNA PRESS
NEW YORK

ACKNOWLEDGEMENTS

The artwork in this book is presented in co-operation with the Lerner-Heller Galleries, New York, New York. The present form of this book is made possible through the support of Elias Bokhara, the Lerner-Heller Galleries, Noble J. Nassar, and Marvin Surkin.

Photography: Leon Yost
Book Design: Bill Plympton
Copyright © by Dan Georgakas, 1976

First Printing

Smyrna Press
Box 841-Stuyvesant Station
New York, New York 10009

This book is dedicated to my friend,
George Biddle, the late American painter and graphic artist,
for his work
for his writings on art and society
for his contributions to young artists
and for his labors on behalf of the WPA art projects.

TABLE OF CONTENTS

INTRODUCTION

The appearance of Nicholas Sperakis—a young, child-like face embellished with a luxurious beard—belies his inner life, full of turmoil, anxieties and passion. That inner life finds expression in his work.

In a former studio on the Bowery, actually a room in a "hotel" for the denizens of that area, he painted (cemented rather, for I would call his technique a kind of "tachism"—he mixes bees'-wax, hot linseed oil, pearlite with his paints) figures of derelicts in dark interiors, lonely, alienated, deteriorated individuals with rotting flesh and clothes.

At present his studio is in a corner building, one flight up, with huge windows offering two exposures: toward the east is the overflow of Chinatown and toward the south is a view all the way to the Municipal Building. The corner seethes with movement, sound and color, and when the windows are open, it is like being outside. All this affects the work he does now—kaleidoscopic, much more colorful than what he did on the Bowery.

A major part of his art are his graphics—the series of huge woodcuts on the human condition such as alienation of man, corruption in organized religion, superstitution, the obscenities of war, life and death. He is driven to this content, he told me, by his desire to escape his fanatically religious childhood background, dominated by taboos, superstition, sexual suppression.

Both in content and technique one can trace influences of the Catalan frescoes, Durer, Cranach, Munch as well as George Grosz and Otto Dix. He spoke to me with great love of the Spanish painters—El Greco and Velasquez, and especially of Goya, who, as Sperakis said, is "the Father of us all."

Raphael Soyer.

The Chanter, 32 x 72 inches, 1963.

Tortured Figurehead In Black Shroud, 20 x 30 inches, 1963.

Standing Monk, 32 x 72 inches, 1963.

Transfigured Portrait Head Of A Youth, 20 x 30 inches, 1964.

The Non-Believing Demon, 7 x 11 inches, 1964.

The Hanging One, 42 x 60 inches, 1964.

21

The Cripple, 42 x 72 inches, 1964.

The Monk, 42 x 72 inches, 1964.

Drawn Upon Palm, 8 x 12 inches, 1964.

The Manias, 32 x 72 inches, 1964.

The Bozzo, 32 x 72 inches, 1964.

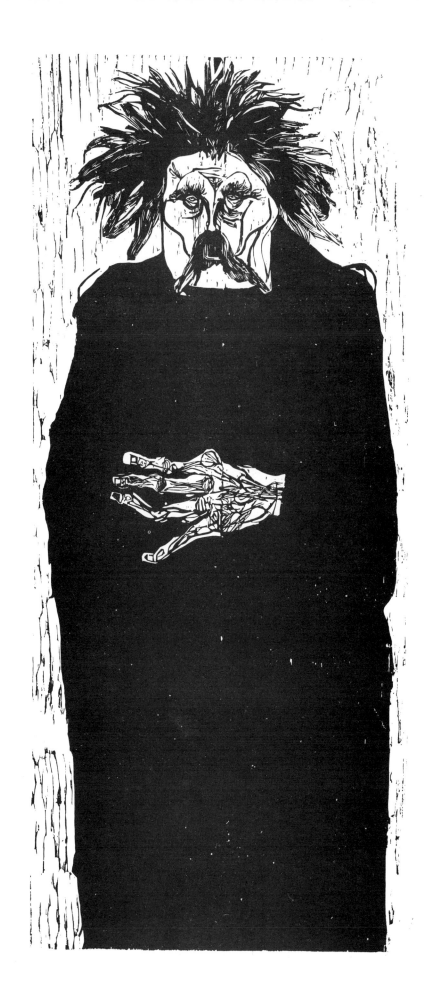

The Crucifixion In The Flesh, 32 x 72 inches, 1965.

The Priest, 32 x 72 inches, 1965.

The Transfigured Transformation, 6 x 12 inches, 1965.

The Metamorphosis, 7 x 12 inches, 1965.

Three Came Once, 10 x 15 inches, 1965.

Death, 32 x 72 inches, 1965.

Terrible Occurence, 5 x 9 inches, 1966.

Violent Aftermath, 42 x 72 inches, 1966.

Genocidal Furnace, 8 x 11 inches, 1967.

Duppuret (From Marat/Sade), 7 x 11 inches, 1967.

Reconsidered Transfiguration, 6 x 10 inches, 1967.

Inmate Of The Asylum of Charenton (From Marat/Sade), 6 x 12 inches, 1967.

The Masked Landscape Of Him, 8 x 12 inches, 1967.

Marat Caught In The Floorboards Just Before His Nightmare (From Marat/Sade), 8 x 12 inches, 1967.

59

The Rape Of Death, 9 x 12 inches, 1968.

Mauthausen Face, 6 x 9 inches, 1964.

42nd Street Fun House, 32 x 64 inches, 1969.

Mr. and Mrs. ?, 30 x 45 inches, 1970.

The Helmeted Queen's Nightmare Fetish, 6 x 9 inches, 1974.

Death Watching, 8 x 12 inches, 1964.

Watching Over, 15 x 20 inches, 1965.

Testament, 10 x 18 inches, 1965.

Leave Him In Peace, 8 x 12 inches, 1965.

Untitled (based on a madrigal by Carlos Gesauldo de Venerosa), 8 x 11 inches, 1967.

The Vision, 32 x 91 inches, 1972.

Tigress In The Night (based on a poem by Frances O'Keefe), 6 x 11 inches, 1972.

Amos (based on a poem by Roderick Faber), 7 x 10 inches, 1972.

Transition Without Stripes, 8 x 11 inches, 1973.

LIST OF WOODCUTS

Page

(all woodcuts done in a series of 40)

Interview with Nicholas Sperakis

The following interview is the result of five taped interviews conducted late in 1975. The interviews took place in the artist's present studio which is located in the vicinity of Chinatown in New York City. Each session lasted approximately an hour. The tapes were then transcribed and the artist and interviewer worked out the final form which appears below. The interviewer, Dan Georgakas, has written extensively on cultural problems and current affairs. He is the author of three books and is currently an associate editor of Cineaste, a film quarterly.

Georgakas: Your series of woodcuts dealing with Greek Orthodox subjects seems to be as hostile to the Greek community as it is to the church. The two have been so closely identified for centuries an attack on one appears to be an attack on both.

Sperakis: I did that series because of an environment I was very intimate with, an environment which had a strong and fanatical obsession with institutionalized religion. It's not a reaction to any one community but to any community confined by institutions which restrict and limit group and personal development. We must also understand that sometimes we allow ourselves to be so limited and restricted. We are responsible, in part, for the continuation of such limitations. We have to understand the apparatus if we want to change. I'm not dealing with one church or one ethnic group. I'm dealing with a state of mind. I call it the Thanatos Series, a series about different kinds of death and death making.

Georgakas: Although you have little nudity and almost no overt sexual images, the Thanatos Series seems permeated with sexual concern.

Sperakis: I think the strongest element in the church is sexual repression, especially with regard to women. I'm not interested in doing pornography; I seek the inner mind. I seek the psyche. I find that church mythology is stronger in its satanic fury than in its serenity or heavenly goodness. I see the church as diabolic and corrupt, using its power to control and maintain people in ignorance. But I want to emphasize that my work is not to be taken as abstract ideology. It is about people acting out a drama.

Georgakas: Your work can be difficult to live with. It's full of forboding and contains much torment and cruelty. Even the actual cutting often seems harsh and negative.

Sperakis: Isn't a religious situation of the Greek Orthodox variety one of great cruelty? In fact, it is one of sadism. They try to control the bodies and minds of people in a restrictive and repressive manner. My woodcuts show people caught up in circumstances which deform them.

Georgakas: Your series on Marat/Sade seems to explore a similar theme.

Sperakis: That's true. I attended the Peter Brook production of the play performed by the Royal Shakespearean Theater of Stratford. I was totally taken up with the images of the play. I've always been strongly influenced by theater and that play was very rich visually. I liked its ritualism, its masks, and its plays within the play. The Marat/Sade work deals with struggle, opposition, and contradiction. It is clearly more symbolic than the Greek woodcuts and apparently more socially oriented because of the characters of Marat and de Sade.

Georgakas: Are you the advocate of Marat or of de Sade?

Sperakis: I understand the argument of de Sade but I move to the solutions of Marat. I must admit that this movement is with great conflict and tortuous dismay.

Georgakas: Artists who deal with the horrors of our age often seem to enjoy the cruelty they say they despise. They become part of the spectacle of cruelty.

Sperakis: I think there is much truth to that observation. An artist can fall into that error. Artists may consciously exploit the grotesque for gain or they may be captured by it. Some people feel that a statement cannot be made unless all traditional forms and values are discarded, that they must go to the canvas with knives and sledge hammers to rent asunder everything we know. Aesthetically and philosophically, I'm opposed to that conception. I don't think that it is human. I think art succeeds most effectively when it deals with the power of suggestion and when it explores various angles of accessibility. A lot of the other stuff is just vulgar literalism. In my own case, I am interested in much more than grotesquery. I try to show what is real. I use the medium to develop various aspects of the horror around us. The work becomes a thing of beauty if it is able to win involvement with the human elements which are left within the horror or by the human response illicited by what is depicted.

Georgakas: What are some of the contradictions and horrors brought out in Marat/Sade?

Sperakis: People like to see themselves as one thing so much that they become oblivious to how they really look or feel. The circumstance of that contradiction brings about a tortured state within themselves that comes through in their faces and bodies without them necessarily being aware of it. I've always been intrigued by masks. A face is usually a mask. It reveals what people don't want revealed about themselves or are afraid to reveal. Masks are often easy to spot. A group of masks becomes a carnival, a human sideshow of errors, misconceptions, absurdities, ironies. Marat/Sade takes place in an insane asylum where the atmosphere is rich in masks and subterfuge. People play the roles they once dreamed or dreaded their real lives might become.

Georgakas: Your monks are so frenzied looking they too could be part of that asylum.

Sperakis: Their asylum is the church. I believe history is an integral part of the creative process. Certain symbols recur in mythology even across widely separated cultures. I often put traditional symbols in a contemporary setting. The priest and the chalice refer to the eucharist which goes back to the cannabilistic devouring of god found in so many mythologies. We've always had these fantasies. I have a serpent coming up out of the chalice in one woodcut as some kind of sexual comment, but I didn't work it out consciously. As I was cutting the chalice, I felt a serpent belonged there too. Much of my work develops that way, in the actual cutting, intuitively. The more you think about symbols consciously, the more sterile and contrived they become.

Georgakas: One of your Greek nuns holds a bouquet of wilted wheat.

Sperakis: Those are dead strands, warped dreams. I find irony and absurdity in such tragedies, even humor. The drama of cruelty is often undercut by folly, a bitter kind of humor. I think of her as a nun and as a widow as well. She is an isolated individual completely confined and alienated, a disassociated soul shrouded within the darkness she's dependent on. The wheat comes from the traditional notion that the seed must die and fall into the earth before it can be reborn. The death it represents relates to this individual's state of lifelessness. It is impossible to give verbal justice to visual concepts or we would write instead of draw and paint.

Georgakas: Do you prepare preliminary sketches for your woodcuts?

Sperakis: Yes and no. I do studies of the imagery in terms of how it can be constructed in relation to the expression I desire, but I very rarely do actual work on compositions as they might appear on the wood block. That goes on in my mind. Sometimes I'll even alter as I cut. The symbols are usually planned beforehand but as I'm cutting, the idea may develop and change radically as a response to what is happening with the wood.

Georgakas: Why are your woodcuts so large? Most of them are larger than life size and they are always in black and white.

Sperakis: I've always been impressed by the effect of monumental scaling. That's one reason why murals have such impact. Of course, if you make an error that becomes monumental too. My themes are partly developed by the relationship my images have to the space they have to contend with. The reason I stay with black and white is that I agree with those who see more "color" in the warm and cold variations achieved by going from black to white than in the variety of inks and other pigments available. The "color" is partly achieved through the cutting process as well. The texture is part of the "gray" of the work. The nature of the wood surface plays another important role in the final effect. Pigments would not advance the themes or enhance the moods I try to convey in the woodcut medium.

Georgakas: When you had a studio near the Bowery your work was filled with images of derelicts.

Sperakis: That studio had a profound effect on me. I always react to my immediate environment. For whatever reasons, those individuals on the Bowery were deteriorating and allowing themselves to deteriorate and wanting themselves to deteriorate. They preyed on one another. I saw many physical horrors of the most repellent nature, yet it was quite normal there. I felt compelled to react. What I put on woodblock existed then and still exists today, but people are willing to accept it. That's the most grotesque aspect of all.

Georgakas: Your bums are never humorous. There's no sense of "Hallelujah, I'm a bum!"

Sperakis: I'm glad you've touched on that. All too often a certain public views them that way which is a complete fallacy. There is nothing to idealize in the total degradation I could view daily from my window. The debased state of these people is not some-

90

thing they bring on themselves in the manner of the legendary hobo, if such a person ever existed. You see them with rags in their hands wiping the windows of cars stopped for a traffic light. You see them crash to the sidewalk in a stupor. You see the dirty rags on their wounds, their broken mouths, their disconnected eyes. In the summer, they are covered with vermin and in the winter, they often freeze to death. The only reason I had that studio for as long as I did was that it was one of the few I could afford at that time.

Georgakas: Is there any connection between the Bowery Series and the Thanatos Series?

Sperakis: They both deal with cripples. And in each series, the victim is the one who becomes a victimizer who takes advantage of others. The inflicted wounds of the sadist turn the victim into a victimizer. It becomes a self-cycling sadism and violence.

Georgakas: You've been classified as a New Humanist, yet your work deals with ritualized murder, insanity, torture, debasement. How do you reconcile that with your humanistic motives?

Sperakis: I am completely opposed to cruelty, sadism, and brutality. That is why I deal with the kind of material I deal with. There is a method we alluded to earlier that real guts and real blood should be used in art. Some people slay real animals on the stage. That reminds me of the geek in the carnival who bites off the head of a live chicken. I am totally opposed to that attitude. It lacks all subtlety and aesthetic value. My work is about people at war with themselves. I would like to see us win that war but the battles are awesome and it is the battles I deal with.

Georgakas: During the period of the recent Greek dictatorship (1967-74) you did a lot of work on behalf of anti-junta groups. You did leaflets, book covers, phonograph album covers—all kinds of things. You've told me that you're not altogether happy with that work.

Sperakis: I don't think art and politics go hand in hand so easily. They want to be lovers but they find it most difficult. The most successful example of this genre is the Horrors of War by Goya who is the Father of us all. He knew that if art preaches, it fails. It cannot be just a poster. Art must have an ideal, explicit or implicit, of how people would like to be. I like to deal with human beings as if they were still capable of ideals. In the junta work I tried to avoid stereotypes. I tried to employ some of our folkloric traditions, but I'm fearful that all of us who worked during that period under that tension and pressure were overly literal. The black and white of the woodcut medium and the skeletal figures were important for they could serve both as metaphoric and naturalistic images for the barbarism of the junta. But you recognize reference points such as uniforms. It will be interesting to see how well that work holds up with time.

Georgakas: Does art change anything, in the political sense?

Sperakis: Art doesn't bring out the voters for candidates x or z. Art brings forth an experience and enters the knowledge of the viewer, so it helps the individual consider new channels and modes of behavior. One of the reasons there is so much censorship of art is due to the power art has to transform people at the roots, not into some action but in a more generalized manner, in terms of overall attitude and world outlook, in terms of understanding institutions and traditions for what they really are. I think art changes emotions more than it changes specific ideas.

Georgakas: Your latest woodcuts are called the Neon Night Series. You deal with scenes that might take place in rough honky tonk areas like Times Square.

Sperakis: In these works I try to deal with people and nature as they are assaulted by anti-nature. Certain elements in technology disturb me. By anti-nature I mean that which imposes and violates, that which distorts. In my work I show figures that have become components of manufacturing processes. They are similar to neon in that they shed light but have no warmth. They are turned on and off, like robots. They are motionless but appear to move. I try to depict the conflict between machine nature and animal nature, the cannibalism of our times. The faces usually contradict the bodies. They appear as separate units at times. They are means of exposing what the person doesn't want exposed. They are masks. The way I depict the hair it looks as if it were shot through with electricity. It is frenzied and chaotic. The figures no longer sit or stand. They are in a gravitational free fall which is not at all graceful. They have nothing to hold them up anymore. There is no recognizable up or down. I am trying to show helplessness with regards to having no control over how one approaches the world.

Georgakas: In one of the Neon Night pieces, a man who is smoking a cigar looks like George Meany. Is that intentional?

Sperakis: It's funny you should say that because I wasn't consciously thinking of George Meany when I began work, but there is a connection. The day before I started on the woodcut I happened to be watching television which is something I rarely do. An interview came on regarding price controls and a wage freeze. Then along came George Meany, this "leader" of the American working class. Well, the president of the AFL-CIO was sitting at one of those Miami Beach hotels announcing an increase in his own salary which already ran to six figures. I found him repulsive and obscene. Perhaps, in some subliminal fashion, the next day he appeared on the block.

Georgakas: Your men seem more hateful than your women. Is this some feminist principle you have?

Sperakis: I don't know anything about feminist principles. The feminists can talk better about that than I can, but I do see men as being more fetishistic and more prone to wear uniforms. I generally draw them in angular geometric forms. They are trapped in the paraphernalia of fetishism. How people dress displays their state of mind. My men often assume the faces of animals which are not recognizable as part of the normal zoological order. My women, on the other hand, are often formed out of many circles. I have these circles on their buttocks, their breasts, their arms. They are bands and stripes. They are mechanical and organic at the same time. There is the anatomical function which is good and the mechanical which is bad. The uterus and the ball bearing socket are both suggested simultaneously. My figures need not be thought of as sexually male or female. One type has its mask painted right on the anatomy while the other type has an animal face and a uniform. I have one couple where I've bequeathed the female type with a penis. That's a couple I actually know.

Georgakas: As in your other woodcuts, in the Neon Night Series you tend not to show the actual sexual parts.

Sperakis: Isn't that the nature of mechanical games? People are so involved in tricks, especially when it comes to sexuality. Real motives get camouflaged or come from some distorted place instead of from where we expect them to come from. The sexual initiative can take a frenzied form which is barely recognizable as sexual at all. I try to find the reality beneath our masquerade of civility. I don't have to be literal because I don't see any advantage to that. Sexual excess is one reality of our times that I don't particularly encourage or find very healthy. Because I use recognizable forms doesn't mean I need to be photographic. We have cameras for that.

Georgakas: Much of contemporary arts deals with art itself and not about people or the real world. The kind of work you do is out of what is conventionally thought of as the mainstream of contemporary North American art.

Sperakis: I don't know what the future will consider our mainstream or sidestream or whatever to have been, and I'm not too concerned with that. I don't think the kind of art you refer to is art at all. When poetry is about how to write a poem and when painting is about how to paint and when film making is about film making, etcetera, etcetera, it becomes pseudo. It doesn't breathe. It doesn't derive from life and it doesn't move to life. It is anti-human because it is about an alienated process. Most of that trend is something which is about and for the sake of nothing. It doesn't even reach the level of the obvious. There is the idea that people will bring their own experiences to the work and use it as terms of reference for their own creativity. That sounds fine but it's just not very interesting most of the time. Why bother with it? People who do that kind of work avoid the responsibility of being a creator with a viewpoint. My work is in an entirely different direction. I think the kind of work I do reaches back to our sources and also reaches forward. I don't like to talk about it too much, however, because such talk always sounds pretentious.

BIOGRAPHICAL NOTES

1943
Born on June 8th in New York City.

1960-63
Studies at the National Academy of Design, the Pratt Graphic Art Center, and the Art Students League of New York. In 1963 exhibits in Annual Print Exhibition of Mercyhurst College, Pennsylvania and wins First Prize Purchase Award. Also has one man exhibition at Paul Kessler Gallery, Provincetown, Mass. Begins work on Thanatos Series which will include 40 woodcuts, 140 drawings, and 45 paintings.

1964
Elected to Society of American Graphic Artists. Exhibits in Annual Print Exhibition of Mercyhurst College, in Brooklyn Museum Print Biennial, and in "New Acquisitions" of Chrysler Museum of Provincetown. Five major works purchased for permanent collection of Walter P. Chrysler Museum. One man exhibition at Paul Kessler Gallery and Hinckley and Brohel Galleries.

1965
Exhibits in Society of American Graphic Artists Annual Graphic Exhibition, Associated American Artists Gallery, New York; "New Acquisitions" of Norfolk Museum of Arts and Sciences, Norfolk, Va. One man exhibitions at Paul Kessler Gallery and Eric Schindler Galleries. "The Beggar" purchased by New York Public Library for its permanent collection.

1966
Exhibits in "One Hundred Prints from the Graphic Arts Center" at Jewish Museum, New York. One man exhibition at Marl Galleries, Woodstock, New York and at Paul Kessler Gallery. Begins work on Marat/Sade Series which will include 15 woodcuts, 91 drawings, and 30 paintings.

1967
One man exhibition of Marat/Sade works at Marl Galleries, Larchmont, New York. Exhibits and is purchased in Brooklyn Museum Print Biennial. Purchased for permanent collection of Norfolk Museum of Arts and Sciences.

1968
One man exhibition at Marl Galleries and Paul Kessler Gallery. One man graphics exhibition at New York University. Teaches graphics at Educational Alliance in New York. Begins Bowery Series which will include 40 woodcuts, 100 drawings, and 35 paintings.

1969
Represented in Candidates for Fellowships and Grants in the Arts and Winners of Fellowships in the Arts and Newly Elected Members of the American Academy and National Institute of Arts and Letters, New York; Lawrence and Hinda Rosenthal Award, American Academy and National Institute of Arts and Letters. One man exhibition at Paul Kessler Gallery. Purchased for permanent collection of Philadelphia Museum of Fine Arts. Travels extensively in Mexico. Begins Neon Night Series which is still in progress.

1970
Guggenheim Fellowship in Printmaking. Travels in Europe. Represented in Brooklyn Museum Print Biennial. Participates in organizing the Rhino Horn artist group which first exhibits at the New School for Social Research, New York. Represented in Rhino Horn exhibits held at Sonraed Gallery in New York, Ohio Art Center in Dayton, Oklahoma State College, Oklahoma State University, and Oklahoma Fine Arts Center. One man exhibition at Paul Kessler Gallery. Represented in "One Hundred Prints from the Pratt Graphic Arts Center" at Jewish Museum. Teaches art at YMHA in New York. Invited by Efram Tavoni, Manager of Contemporary Art International Exhibitions of Bologna, Italy and Mrs. Louis Bingham, Chief of the International Art Program, Washington D.C. and Professor Toni Spiteris, Secretary General of the A.I.C.A. of Paris in conjunction with the International Poard of Art Critics, to participate in a number of major print exhibitions in the leading museums of France, Italy, Spain, other parts of Europe, and the Far East (1970-71).

1971

One man exhibitions at Long Island University (Brooklyn), the Pratt Institute Manhattan Center, the Paul Kessler Gallery, and the Sonraed Gallery. Represented in Annual Print Exhibition of Honolulu Academy of Fine Arts and in "Protest Prints" sponsored by the Pratt Graphic Arts Center, Columbia University. Rhino Horn exhibits in New York City, University of Hartford, and Bienville Gallery in New Orleans. Teaches at Brooklyn Museum Art School.

1972

One man exhibition at Paul Kessler Gallery. Second Rhino Horn exhibit at Sonraed Gallery. Teaches painting at New School for Social Research.

1973-74

Participates in "Voices of Alarm" exhibit at Lerner-Heller Gallery in New York. Woodblock exhibition at Pace University Gallery and one man exhibition at Paul Kessler Gallery. Group exhibition at Aida Hernandez Gallery in New York and Artemis East Gallery in New York. Rhino Horn exhibitions: Rabinovitch-Guerra Gallery in New York, Ankrum Gallery in Los Angeles, Aida Hernandez Gallery, and Chrysler Museum in Norfolk, Virginia.

1975

One man exhibition at Lerner-Heller Gallery, Paul Kessler Gallery, and Bienville Gallery. "The Vision" purchased for permanent collection of Oklahoma Art Center. Series of "portraits" done with sitters is begun.

1976 (through February)

A second one man exhibition is planned at the Lerner-Heller Gallery as well as participation in the group exhibit called "A Patriotic Show" also at Lerner-Heller Gallery.

This book, *The Woodcuts of Nicholas Sperakis*, was printed in New York City in 1976. The edition has been limited to one thousand copies. The first five hundred are numbered and signed by the artist. The first ten copies are in Roman numerals. They contain an original drawing and an original woodcut by the artist. Copies eleven through forty are also in Roman numerals. They contain an original woodcut by the artist. The book was designed by Bill Plympton. The printing was done at Photo Comp in New York City.